How to Make
Cheese Muffins

Written by Isabel Bissett
Illustrated by Brenda Costeloe

Read the recipe.
Wash your hands ready to begin.

You will need these utensils:

a mixing bowl
a measuring cup
a tablespoon
a wooden spoon
a muffin tray (for 12)
a knife
a plate

You will need these ingredients:

2 cups of self-raising flour
2 cups of grated cheddar cheese
1½ cups of milk
butter (to grease the muffin tray,
    and for spreading)
salt

Collect everything you need.
Grease the muffin tray.

Move the oven rack to the middle position, and turn the oven on to 350° Fahrenheit.

Measure 2 cups of self-raising flour.
Pour it into the mixing bowl.
Add a pinch of salt.

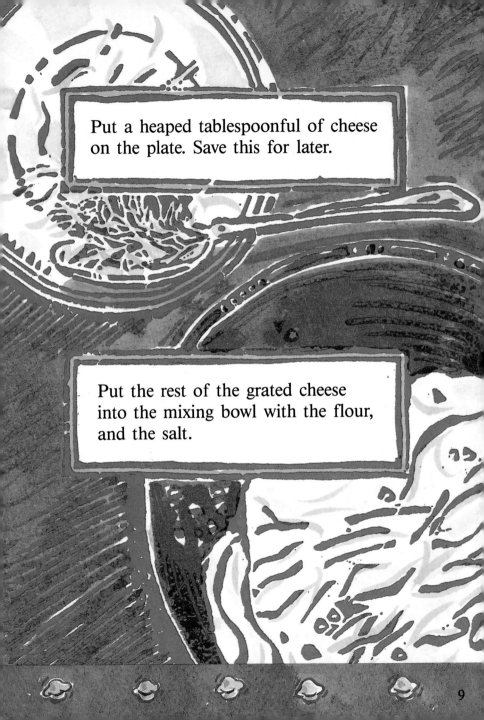

Put a heaped tablespoonful of cheese on the plate. Save this for later.

Put the rest of the grated cheese into the mixing bowl with the flour, and the salt.

Measure 1½ cups of milk.
Add this to the flour, cheese, and
salt in the bowl.

Mix well, using the wooden spoon.

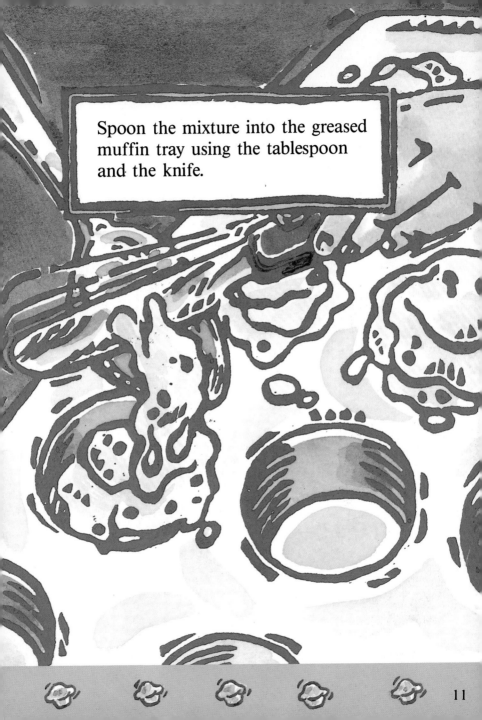

Spoon the mixture into the greased muffin tray using the tablespoon and the knife.

Put the muffins in the oven.
Bake them for 20 minutes.

Take the muffins out of the oven.
Use oven gloves.

Allow the muffins to cool slightly, then tip them into a bread basket.

Serve them warm, with butter.